Interactive Press

Flaubert's Drum

*Born and raised in Malaysia, Sugu Pillay has postgraduate degrees from Victoria University of Wellington and the University of London. Awarded a Creative New Zealand Grant in 1997, she completed her collection of short fiction, **The Chandrasekhar Limit**, which was published by The Writers Group, Auckland in 2002. In 2009, her play, **Serendipity**, premiered in Wellington. Her second play, **Salaam Pukekohe**, was co-winner of Playmarket's 2010 **Write Out Loud** script development programme. **Flaubert's Drum** (previous title: **In Medias Res**) highly commended in 'IP Picks Best Poetry 2012', is a collection of mostly published poems from 1995 to 2012. A former resident of Christchurch, Sugu now lives in Wellington.*

Interactive Press
The Literature Series

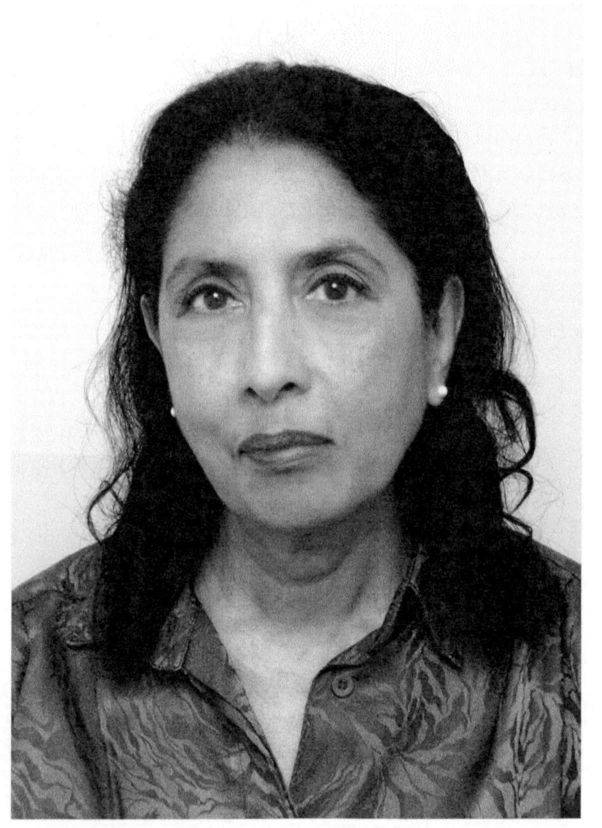

Flaubert's Drum

Sugu Pillay

Interactive Press
Brisbane

Interactive Press
an imprint of IP (Interactive Publications Pty Ltd)
Treetop Studio • 9 Kuhler Court
Carindale, Queensland, Australia 4152
sales@ipoz.biz
ipoz.biz/IP/IP.htm

First published by IP in 2012
© Sugu Pillay, 2012

Printed in 12 pt Cochin on 16 pt Bell Gothic Std.

National Library of Australia
Cataloguing-in-Publication entry:

Author: Pillay, Sugu.

Title: Flaubert's drum / Sugu Pillay.

ISBN: 9781921869945 (pbk.)

Dewey Number: NZ821.3

Acknowledgements

Front Cover Image: dreamstime.com

Jacket Design: David Reiter

Author Photos: James Gilberd

Thanks to the editors of *Takahe, Printout, Voiceprints 2, A Brief Description of the Whole World/brief, Bravado, Spin, The Christchurch Press, JAAM, Poetry NZ* and online journals, *Trout, Fugacity* and *a fine line* where most of these poems were first published. Some have been revised for this collection.

Contents

Flaubert's Drum

*Writers have to have two countries, the one where they belong
and the one in which they live really.*

– Gertrude Stein.

Mission Bay to St Heliers

Mission Bay

She steps on rotting seaweed
crunched shells bloated bells
her wet feet scoop space
a landscape the width of a glance
gulls with staring eyes
circle restlessly overhead
the heat is everywhere
even in the cool crystals
rising in the air over the sea
in daring stained glass allure
its memory embedded
in collapsing waves
memory & myth, *theatrum mundi*
this is how the world gets lighter
no matter what the story
of the Bay seething in its rays
its waters to the brim
& not a drop spilled

Joggers, stomach sucked in
nostrils flaring hair whistling
circle a coastline taken root
in pohutukawa red
picnickers wild with sun in their eyes
toast the good life with plastic wine
Rangitoto keeps watch
now as in Heaphy's watercolour
not black lava, not red sky
just green, remote, forbidding

had it not witnessed *The Platina*
sail into the Waitemata harbour
with the Governor's house on board?
this foreign body in its eye!

She sits down framed
by *umbrageous foliage*
Picasso's beached woman
embracing the body of the sea
its fish, loaves & flotsam
eyes wide open & wanting words

Tradition & the Poet I

oaring (their) way through sun-lanced waters
the surfers speed

the placing of objects
a crucial act in geodesic space
she strives for more contact
her index finger moves, stretches
till it touches these abstractions
of line, colour, movement
& having moved she arcs
to adapt this scarlet coastline
for her savage survival

everything takes shape
in a Shakespearean billowed belly
always love shivers & puckers
out there beyond where white sails
dip in dip out picking up the good phrase
a cult of the Sorrows
the image strikes
bites the hand that gives it life

sitting is a way of life
sitting on the words of the other
sitting on eggs that never hatchbreak
but break on long stretches of sand
& time running out

summon the poet's sister
for whosoever would browse
the eloquence of space
an infinity of cat strings
circle the grounded boat

where is Claudia Quinta?
she who dressed too elegantly
unchaste woman who argued with men
will she step yet again into Tiber's mouth
pull ashore through yielding mudbanks
the prophetess, warrior queen, matriarch?

dare the labyrinth backwards
break off the bough
through Alice's mirror
savour the romance

Nausicaa in bits of red dye
dilates in tiny blue flames
Aphrodite's butterfly gaze
remembers, anticipates, mutates
Homer's ventriloquist voice
speaking names aloud in mouthfuls
of purloined air wakes gods, heroes
& the waiting woman

Assimilation of History

(A Reading of Una Platts' *The Lively Capital*, 1971)

She renews her walk
close to the pohutukawas
sweet beneath their bleeding hearts
her heart flapping butterfly wide
while the flamingo hour flutters

Lunchers in the Mission Restaurant
toss in creamed scallops
then circle the Fountain of Life
to the silent roar of straining merlions

La vita e bella

So thinks Bishop Selwyn as he trots
towards Kohimarama Mission
replete with cake & wine
at the Bambridges

As he rounds the Bay
the Bishop catches his breath
light & water bouncing off each other
the entire coastline aflame
Kohimarama
Gathering in of light!
He wishes the landscapists would leave off
their browns, greens, greys of the old world
that they dip their brushes in gold & Madonna blue
Would he ever get used to this oceanic bounty?

He falls to musing about Bunbury's Tamaki farm
a labour of love in carrots as *thick as a man's legs*
turnips *the size of a man's head*
Italian corn as tall as Bunbury himself
pumpkins, marrows, cucumbers
& that prized Egyptian wheat!
A pity about the Te Kawau affair
now the Taylors have taken over
with wistful names for each new farm
Glen Innes, Glendowie…

Soon the Bishop is in the Mission grounds
home for his beloved Solomon Island boys
ready to return to their country good Christians
what a trump Paterson turned out to be
looks after the boys most conscientiously
*cartloads of pipi shells under the wooden floors
the scoria wall to keep out the south wind*
poor blighters they hate the winters!

The Bishop bounds up the stairs
to take his turn with the nursing
damn the dysentery!
He's determined not to lose
any more of his boys

History & Cultural Relativity

Joggers, *heedless extras,* pause for breath
watch the waters wind round her unruly brush
in four or five shifts in perspective

The hills are dark adventurous
wooing strong thoughts
with the gathering cumulous
& sea-brackish wraiths

The sea trembles & heaves
its deep flat no longer neutral
in cinematic sweeps it *kicks and bites
and fights* crafts and swimmers

Faraway figures totter
in *graceful conciliatory gestures*
they fall in heaps
disconnected souls
amidst wobbling waves
a Brueghel frenzy of the global village
& one dimensional man

Meremere…Rangiriri…Orakau
ka whawhai tonu ake! Ake! Ake!
would the breach ever be healed?
Bishop Selwyn holds in his arms
a casualty of that hateful battle at Orakau
tenderly he attends to his wounds
(habouring *the Queen's enemies!*)

Selwyn knows this old friend in his arms
will surely die of his wounds
they die in the belief they'd overcome
we die in the belief we know best
us...them...

He mea nei hoki au ka pakaru rikiriki
te waka ki taku akau

Lament

Heat clings to the cliffs
relishing the prospect of drownings
as it must have on the day
Wairaka set eyes on Rangikitua
chief of the Waioha people of Tamaki

There's Rangi now on that rocky outcrop
a melancholy flute on his lips
well, now that we have seen each other
if you'll believe in me, I'll believe in you
Does he puzzle over Mai & Wairaka?
Suddenly he leaps up
& renders in furious roar
a haka to deceit
its many faces & voices

Po, po, po Wairaka i raru ai
more heart-rending than Apakura's lament
Wairaka's cry echoes back from Whakatane
to the crimson indifference of this coastline

       An open Beckett-mouth hangs in space
       its rehearsed lines of streaming semi-colons
       out to sea & at sea

       all sails disappear in the mist
       of the willful

       text of contested space
       locked in the traceless waiting
       of circled water

Person & Place

The waves break
    In eternal call to the pohutukawas
Two redbills flap down
    In their dive
Dürer's passions large & small

Having sent all scrambling back to shore
    The sea thunders in
Digging holes in the sand
    Like turtles about to lay eggs

This could be the very spot
        Taurere!
Where the great canoe Aotea
    Beached one stormy night
These the shores
    Where the historic gift
Of Hawaiki kumara took place
    & the gift of the karaka berries
From Turanga to Parehuia

Alas, this is also an accursed shore
    Where pohutukawas shed their shame
All along the running beach
    Sad the maiden who sees her father
Slain at the hands of her lover
    & her lover slain in weary battle
So far from home

Somewhere in the Ruahini ranges
    Te Ahu ki Turangaimua
Marks the spot he fell
    He hono tangata e koro e mohi

Somewhere …
    In the virtual reality of Taurere
There's a gnarled karaka tree
    From its branches hang
The whitened bones of Parehuia

            She looks up
            The starless sky

            Stars do not die
            The everchanging forms
            Of dust & gas swirl

            Take abode in one body
            Then take off again

            Atoms like troubadours
            Take their stories
            From body to body

            Affirming the ties
            Between person & place

In Medias Res

In tumbled sport the sea collects
stories from shore to shore
drawing in with a kiss
running out with the tide

It's on these mythic shores
she chose to make her home
...... *a vagrant, a player*
who holds nothing & whom nothing holds
granted only, by a questionable sea,
to gaze at the land of (her) choice

Here, Sargon of Akkad
here, Horus, here Moses, here Karna
all set adrift by their mothers in waters
laden with the world's stories

This could also be the shore
the boats set sail to drop triangular cakes
for fish to nibble

Ch'u Yuan's leaping fish hum softly
flaunting tensions distributing seeds
of *die gestundetete*

The ancient & the now walk in step
the past collapsing over the present
I wait & wait till you
blow my mate to me

Kannaki stands in the shadows
Kovalan & Matavi exchange verses
on the enigma of clause embedded love
their delirious tongues fly across
the open wound of a cleft breast

Ilanko floats up

With bloated indignant eyeball
commands a proper telling
of the moral (sting?) in the tale

*(articulation is but a plank
over the abyss)*

Tradition & the Poet II

Re: A 5th Century Epic of South India
(Making Free With Parthasarathy's 1993 Translation)

Great literature knows
Love may require one to bury
The Beloved's head in a pot of basil
That love knows no narrative
But that of double-speak

The sliding word dances
dissolves and rematerializes
to describe this region
of otherness and desire

It's the first day of Spring
The full moon is in Virago
The resplendent city of Puhar
Wakes to its annual Festival of Indra
Streets begin to overflow
With princes, royal councilors,
Courtiers, noble merchants,
Horsemen, charioteers

King Muchukuntan of Chola dynasty
Bears in procession the auspicious drum
To the Temple of the White Elephant
Oboes, harps, tambourines
Chants of priests and bards fill the air

A lone woman dressed in her maid's clothes
And a veil over her face emerges
From a mansion in the boulevard
Where merchant princes dwell

She is Laksmi herself goddess
Of peerless beauty that rose from the lotus
And chaste as the immaculate Arundhati

Kannaki walks rapidly past homes
Of brahmins and landed gentry
Physicians, astrologers and astronomers
Great musicians, bards and panegyrists
Till she comes to the street of dancers
Actresses and courtesans

She looks up
At the gaily festooned balconies
Which was Matavi's?
Matavi whose mastery of five types
Of literary Tamil, four melodic patterns
And eleven kinds of dance by age twelve
Captivated everyone

…In the bedroom
Matavi's couch was sown with homegrown
Mullai petals, musk jasmine
…Undone was her red
Coral girdle that blazed over her mound
Of love, and the fine garment unwound
From her waist

…In the shadows
Kannaki sheds bitter tears
Annihilate but time and space
Erase that infamous dance
That mesmerized Kovalan!

Festival revellers draw near
Young women with painted breasts flee
Half heartedly from broad-chested young men
Perfumed with sandal paste

It was thus Indra's Festival ends
With dances, masquerades and amorous
Encounters
    On the beach
Matavi's servants would erect
The love pavilion for the night's revels
On fine sand a small enclosure
Planted with fragrant pandanus

Perhaps they're there now
Matavi enchanting Kovalan
With her siren songs
Unbearable thought!

Kannaki hurries back
The way she came
(Poetic licence, my dear readers
        Kannaki never did roam far from home
        God forbid!)

As she enters her home
Kannaki is startled
By the grief-stricken face
Of long absent Kovalan
He folds her in his arms
And weeps for forgiveness
Has he come to stay? she asks
No! they're to leave tonight for Maturai
To redeem his honour and lost fortune

Is there anything left? he asks
Only the anklets on her feet, she replies
That'll do, let's away, he urges
Where's Matavi?
This, Kannaki does not ask

Nor does Kovalan narrate
His dramatic exit from
The pavilion on the sand
His footprints washed away
By the *counter-signing* sea
(a parting much celebrated
 in verse and drama)

Thus Kovalan returns
His years of neglect forgiven
And we're told
even the gods adore her
who adores no god
but her husband

Readers, time and fiction
Take their customary leap
We're now in Maturai
Capital city of Pantiya kingdom

And here the denouement gathers speed
Ilanko's *deus ex machina,* the royal goldsmith
Pins his theft of the Queen's anklet
          On Kovalan

The King
          Commands the culprit's death
                    and it's done!

When the news reaches Kannaki
A female Prometheus
(says Parthasarathy)
Bursts forth
        (a scene even more celebrated
        in verse, drama and film)

Hoy, door keeper! Hoy, watchman! Hoy palace guards
Of an irresponsible ruler whose vile heart lightly casts
Aside the kingly duty of rendering justice! Go! Tell
How a woman, a widow, carrying a single ankle
Bracelet from a pair that once joyfully rang together,
Waits at the gate. Go! Announce me!

Admitted to the royal presence
Kannaki smashes to bits her anklet
Rubies and diamonds scatter
In eight directions

Kovalan is not the thief
The Queen's anklet being inlaid
With pearls!

The King clutches his heart
Falls & dies
        ...even Kings, if they break
The laws, have their necks rung by dharma

Kannaki is not so easily appeaced
She rushes out of the palace
Beating her breast wailing vengeance
On the city of Maturai

A fevered imagination sees
Her twist and tear a burning breast
And throw it on to the city
The city bursts into flames
Such is the power say the sages
Of a chaste woman's body
All but the virtuous of Maturai
Burn to cinders

(In *Chandra's Vengeance*, an oral residue
published by John Murray in 1868
it's the Purwari outcastes who're spared

For those who doubt *no text is free of other texts*)

Distraught Kannaki takes refuge
In the forests of the neighbouring
Ceral kingdom

Her ascension to Heaven
On Indra's chariot is witnessed
By the tribe that dwells there

> *A chaste woman with only one breast*
> *Stood in the thick shade of the kino*
> *Tree, incandescent in its golden flowers*

And so a Goddess is born
Hewn from a stone
Of mount Podiyil

> Ilanko faithfully records
> *The choice of a stone*
> *Removing the stone*
> *Lustration of the stone*
> *Installation and dedication*

The Goddess of the Round Stone
Consecrated in a temple built
By the Ceral King Cenkuttuvan
Gives the King divine authority
To declare himself Emperor of the South
And wage war against the Aryan North

Thus poet and Jain monk Ilanko
Adds the obligatory *puram* (the heroic)
To *aham* (the erotic) and *puranam* (the mythical)
Scores a literary victory for the Tamils
And leaves a legacy for

  Zerschreiben!

Caminataiyer resurrects the story in 1892
And revels in Ilanko's astonishing evocation
Of fifth century Tamil landscape
Its flora and fauna
Its music, dance and courtship
Its cities and trade

But the hurl of the severed breast
Is too powerful an image for some
Tankaiya allows the fire that burns Maturai
To originate from a tear Kannaki sheds

Pukalenti to be rid of Ilanko's Jaina bias
Revisions Kannaki as Mother Kali
A force of nature

Paratitacan modernizes and foretells
The birth of New Woman
Way ahead of his time

Karunaniti politicizes the epic and woos
Victory for his Dravidian Progressive Party
A clarion call for Tamil sovereignty

All from a space of permission
Less than two inches wide
In crumbling palmyra leaves
Of eight surviving manuscripts
In circulation for 1400 years

St Heliers

One toe dipping into the black paint
she steps into the canvas
no consoling light
from café windows opposite
where once they held hands
& supped the sea's virtual puns
then a brilliant picture
now a flattened perspective
lovers affirm reality by their flight
into one dimensional borders on Grecian urns
frozen but sustained by *Being-in-Time*

And now the dreamy landscape leaps away
the red runs right through the blue
casting mauve shadows on stars
falling into the drowning sea
as the waves die on her *palette of blobs*

& Time always sets with Robbie Burns
whose June rose spreads its scarlet
in shock waves spinning out
from the darkening Rangitoto

Its once radiant node
the composing eye of this seascape
dims like wounded Bhishma
on his bed of arrows

Swinging in & out of her eyeline
the sails have sunk her gaze
stranded like a pilot whale
on Farewell Spit

*Who rides so late in the night
and wind?*

Galaxies of women…

Virginia's mermaid continues to sit
on her rock *with a pad on her knee*
saving a page for the relentless sea
surging in

Her shadow stretches
from Mission Bay to St Heliers

*The problem of space has not found
its proper articulation*
or that of time's *textes pour rein*
since all movement is towards loss

Beckett artfully transferred stones
from pocket to pocket to the mournful tune
we cannot know & we cannot be known
Virginia would have told him
stones drown in women's pockets

Gallery Talk

Gallery Talk on New Brighton Beach

stones
>   the sculptor's stones line the gallery walls
>   in a symphony of square boxes
>   like riddles from Beckett's pockets
>
>   just one in Virginia's pocket for the leap
>   into water and become the riddle

waiting
>   Beckett wrote a whole play on this
>   had a way with words he did
>   round and round they went
>
>   circling like the sea gulls
>   on this beach

driftwood
>   her figure of driftwood 8
>   does not lie on a gallery floor
>
>   it's building walls around her
>   as she walks New Brighton beach

dying
>   Beckett wrote a lot about dying
>   but it was Virginia who dived
>
>   making Ophelias of us all who ask
>   what lies over Sutton's golden threshold?

Trope

one of life's grenade throwers

walking into a Constable
had the good sense
to disappear in time

untidiness of purpose

if a woman is a river
he put the pain there
Joyce did

touch trope & tryst

for inferred coherence
try a flower plucked
loves me not

a persuasion of the real

we're cells
in the body of God
deconstructing

what does this poem know?

Snow and Josh Groban

White balls of ice
fling themselves down
on my courtyard
sometimes in a sleet
sometimes they crisscross
now they circle as they fall
free to choose
design or chaos
loyal only to poetry
or is it geometry?

Like pop love
they tempt you to join in
& frolic in falling
the whole nine yards

Warm inside
Josh sings
he's let someone go
he's let this person fly
now he's wondering why
the true insider's guide
speaks like geometry
in Greek

Dark of Heart, Dark of Mind

last hill
last light
last joy

a limitless now

last words
posted subversions at half mast
their light like stars
guide the dark passage

last syllable
of recorded time
adventuresome material
from the old world

knowing about craft
as a well-made sail
dipping over the horizon
waiting to be hauled ashore
to a wedding feast

since we don't want to be
as good as dead
love, be that raft
when craft & lyric fail

Flaubert's Drum

that harlequin tear again
its fall threatened in Keats' time

her soapy slippery anguished palms
cup for the reflecting bell-jar

each drop
the world's grammar
the Rosetta stone

plows wide furrows
meets with resistance
may or may not connect
never certain that it should

each known thing easily
becomes unknown

like that cracked kettle
of Flaubert's

Museum of Art

there's a boat
longing for the sea

in the abandoned geographies
of the universe

under the sea
you must love me

a giveaway line
from an unlikely source

a torn papyrus
borders a time
    & the embracers

        her path winding
        unwinds in his tender arms

            melodic moments of bloom

                allow love
                its flowering pleasure

                on Ariel's wings

leaving a woman behind
the epic hero defines himself

Nausicaa

a crystal shift
of the day's eye

petals flag a theory
of the woman in white

the woman as masterpiece

shall we write the Book of Sighs
the sigh migrating from page to page?
shall we play in a quilt craft
of ampersands?

lowered into the fire
wake up inside your head

full frontal picture

memory, death & yes, karma
are all they are cracked up to be

erasure tapes

Strings

1st January 2003

here comes the sun of pop songs
& metaphysical poems
breaking the morning
with its glare & demands
for purposeful activity

no compassed lover
holding me back
        I leap out of bed
determined to make
this day memorable

first the Gayatri mantra
a delirious relentless repetition
like the face of Frida Kahlo
spread out on my coffee table
it roots

You are on Earth
There's no cure for it

I look out
see the Ake ake forsaken
on poor soil

my Kowhai almost six feet high
droops in cascade over the footpath
its promise of gold hijacked
by the Donnish sun winding its way
round the Kashmir/ Cash-mere hills

then without asking
it's made for me by Janet Frame
on her 70th birthday *dunny roses* tribute
"I can write sentences," she says
my *rage for order* is over
for the day

Eo fis

such lofty thoughts I take to bed
with tonight's *The West Wing*

the unfinished pyramid & He
who favours our undertakings

pandas mourn when the loved one dies
daughters lie to the jackal that dances

Yes Minister, Spin City, my friend reassures
spell the difference between cultures & humour

Elizabethan humours?

the dark of the cinema, the dark of its cave
usurped by the flashing knowing box

the scripts get better & better
aye, *the monster is the world*

I resolutely take my book in hand
(we are meant to read books & discuss them)

Nabokov's butterfly details confuse
offer their unique signature on all
the eye sees as noun & verb

what actual gods?

I fall asleep with the reassuring smell
of fish curry on my fingers

The Butterfly & the Crab

Derrida answers his question
Who is writing for Whom?
I don't know

a space of permission
for the butterfly & the crab
free of strings
nothing ties them
down

what do they have in common?
maestro Calvino says they *hurry slowly*
every move unalterable

festina lente!
the crab in its sidelong run
along the rim of *a sunless sea*
computes the square root of epigrams
for *poets-who-have-turned-to-prose*

in a narrative
any object
  is always magic

      in the jungles of Borneo
      the IDEA SP is a grey floppy butterfly
      which covers ground in a flutter
      of chiffon skirts

time takes no time
in a story

     in the annals of China
     Chuang-tzu first took five years
     & then another five
     to paint the perfect crab
     with a single brush stroke

Netting in Hong Kong

the knowledge economy goes round the world
Hong Kong's Octopus bears it on its back

spreading windows faster than the Lady
of the Lake spins mutating webs

(the mirror hasn't cracked yet
the webs haven't flown out)

like China's East Village artists
adding one inch to an anonymous mountain

covered in honey
Nets sigh their way to classes

the Yellow River Lullaby floats by
as they enter the belly of the Octopus

& confront more than eight limbs
no delicate brush painting this

no Hong Kong of the mind
fastened by a *netsuke*

an open fabric knotted
in meshes meant for fish & butterflies

a single theme played against itself
in that infamous crab canon

if Wittgenstein's lion would speak
in a metaphorical fugue
what would it say?

that Odin hung in agony from a tree
to net the Salmon of Knowledge?

Transcendent Harmonies

The sky has spun
its clouds around

Your words thread
a similar course

Trickster sun in and out
all morning

The rain when it comes
does not quench

Raindrops like beads
on clothesline

*Translation is inhaling
the whole*

*And exhaling
transcendent harmonies*

The woman
with five elephants

Is not my aunt
who renders in homespun Tamil

The sonorous Sanskrit
of Valmiki's Ramayana

Strings

school is a four-story
brick & tiled affair

only the blind are free

RIGHT OF ABODE
in Repulse Bay

FALUN GONG
    wanted! room to stand
without casting a shadow

BIRD FLU
70,000 poultry slaughtered

sounds like
poetry haltered

events that rhyme
crushed insects in food dye
beef fat in McDonalds' fries
7 virtues painted on a ceiling
in Minneapolis

think in stitches

THE FAIR CAPTIVE
the twin towers of Petronas
house a new lady

Merlin & Excalibur
await THE GOOD MAN

the windmills tilt & tilt
on ROGUE STATES

inside the whale
in love with the hidden abyss
Chomsky crustaceous & lepidopterous
        reinscribes as often
as is necessary

        only the blind are free
        in a world of stories

A Koan for Hari

dear Hari

I have
a question
for you

which you perforce
must answer
with a definitive
yes or no

not
I don't know
I'm not sure
perhaps

or any other
versions of these

& in return
you can ask
me a question

which I do solemnly
swear to answer
with an unequivocal
eventoned
yes or no

for as you know
from time immemorial
the rules are
it's satori flash the first answer
or nothing
second thoughts
are for nonbelievers

& then, dear Hari
there are those who fear

asking or answering
questions of any kind

be they
the classic butterfly question
or the essence or existence first question
or the sound of onehandclapping question
the question to end all questioning

but dear Hari
my question is none of these
or all of these

what's the answer?
what's the question?

Who Said What

Kowhai Gold

the ceremonial room is large & full
we're all there with our two guests
Michelanne says how nice of you
you're wearing your cultural costume
costume? am I acting a part?

seated between a Sri Lankan & a Vietnamese
one who speaks and one who doesn't
I think of landfall & the contest for space
the diaspora & the *severed tongues*
I realize it's indeed high drama
the moves blocked in Shakespeare's Time
    the greatest wonder?
    we act as if we live forever
    replies Yudhisthira

the Vietnamese has little English
we nod & smile & nod again
I couldn't help wondering
who helped her with the form-filling
what had she chosen for RESPONSIBILITIES?
I had piously settled for *Obey & promote*
    The Laws of New Zealand
    & Not act in a way that is against
    the interests of New Zealand

music fills the auditorium
I sit back to enjoy the dance of welcome
every stamp of foot, every flicker of tongue
writes me into this land
I wasn't driven here by war or famine
or any other threat of death
unlike my deeply engrossed neighbour
        what had she ticked for PRIVILEGES?

a Town Councillor appears on stage
he apologises for the Mayor's absence
& welcomes us to nationhood
he leads our oath of allegiance
our voices rise & fall all around us
not having rehearsed together
we put up with discordance

next the presentation
my neighbour & I rise to take our place
in the queue towards the handshake
each of us receives a Certificate
& a Kowhai seedling
plant it in your garden, watch it grow
await its shower of gold
advises the Councillor

gold? *Kowhai gold?*
my thoughts turn poetic
who was it who wrote
There is nothing here but sad sea water
And a handful of sifting sand?
flying foxes & freedom trees!
is it six degrees of separation?

again I wonder what was her choice
for PRIVILEGES?
after much nailbiting I had ticked
Full Economic Rights
& A New Zealand Passport

full economic rights?

we return to our seats
clutching our seedlings to our hearts
together we examine the label
its information & instructions
we nod & smile & nod
we know what our first act
as obedient citizens will be!

Who Said What

So, you're one of us now
A flightless bird, said Michael
What? I asked, not free
Like a bird on a tree?
Not this bird! He assured me
With some satisfaction, I thought

Freedom, said Iris Murdoch
Does not make you happy
Neither does, she continued
Education

Love does

The Tree in its Setting

The tree has its heart
in its roots
like serpentine twine
holding fast to earth
the trunk astride
Gertrude Stein's two countries

Parched for artful rescue
the heart
its roots in a tree
transplanted

I whanau te kauri i konei

Root shock is trauma
cultural operations release pathogens
waking up in the dead of night
with what am I doing here
uprooting or putting down
esculent roots
so succulent with lazy water
digging trenches too close
to the root system

Steadfastness is not the North Star
nor the Southern Cross
so visible despite dark nights
of the soul
rather a shooting star
in sudden & satori flight
shaping *identity by location*
& stories by relocation

The Tree of Heaven in Christchurch's Botanical Gardens

In my dream
a tree concurs with Emerson
The hours of our life
& the centuries of time
bind inextricably

The Ailanthus
shakes in its shallow roots
sick with butt rot
& an amputated arm

Not far with menacing tentacles
the Duke of Edinburgh's tree
usurps space above & beneath
a blockbuster Raj quartet

I gaze up the spartan arms
of the Tree of Heaven
The sun razzles through leafy nets
drags murky details into light
like Diwali sparklers spotlight faces
given to melancholy

Qui tollis peccata mundi?

Kneeling & inclining
like some Lord of the Rings character
the Tree of Heaven between beds
of fading petunias & cruciferous alyssum
bends to my enquiry as boundlessly
as God offers love & says

Make the text, an Event

*Man is explicable by nothing less
than all his history*

Waking up in Stanley Place, Akaroa

Here where the land greenhumpbacked rises
& drops into Te Rauparaha's murderous sea
purple mists shroud seashore & seabed
seeking unities in the destiny of the word

I wake up in sweet recognition
each syllable a Buddha-heart
stirring & rising a skirl & a whirl
tandava nuclei in free space greater
than all this garrulous geography
striking root in Stanley's flag

With utmost expedition
Mandelstam's *verb on horseback*
gallops round the peninsula
& covertly trafficks with Dante
Et in Arcadia ego

Nine Eleven & Me

you & me eye to eye
in armchair comfort
sway in horror
on towering infernos
fall & forever lose
each other

put on a profile type
my face blinks
as searchlights roam
hungry for prey

in a café queue
for a cup of tea
I sidle towards the cashier
as she smiles & jokes
with those before me
but my highlighted mug
turns hers into stone
I place my order before
The Statue of Liberty

on the Orbiter
full of school children
I stand & sway
over a pair of uniformed eyes
locked on my satchel
clutched in one hand
over my black breast

'Excuse me', she says, dashing
past before the bus halts
the child's fear leaves a cocoon
of rancid smell on me

I am ready
for metamorphosis

arriving on campus
I walk the square
between Library & Registry
an armourguard van
screeches brakes by me
two guards jump out
& look terror in the face
I walk serenely on
clutching my purring
grenade close to me

one quirky day
the library is cordoned off
we are herded crocodile file
away from excited whispers
'a bomb! a bomb!'

my writerly curiosity
gets the better of me
a cop standing sentinel
assures me, 'It's real alright!'
a suspicious package
not a hoax in a campus
full of pranksters?

ten minutes later
my mug is clicked
on a cell phone

why speak when your face
is not your fortune?

I never learn
freedom of speech
is not a rainbow
but a black & white
still life

on a plane
seated by the Exit
I sigh & stretch my furry legs
a flight attendant slides up
asks for my briefcase
I hand it over
another rolls up
asks for my coat & scarf
I surrender these
she asks for my purse
this I refuse
how can I give up
this phantom bomb?

at home
I search my face
for the mark of Cain

Immigrant Song

no, I will not hijack your life
though I climb every mountain
ford every river
cherish every taonga
this land holds sacred

no, I will not plant a bomb
on the banks of the Avon
though willows weep over waters
too shallow to drown

no, I will not bring Avian flu
to *this fair far-flung land*
though I flavour my food
with spices from Asia

no, I will not steal your thunder
though you rain on my parade
play political games
impale my tongue

no, I will not say
Canterbury, take my bones
no, not till I've seen
the fabled *nor'west arch*
streak across the sky
a new covenant
for *this other Eden*

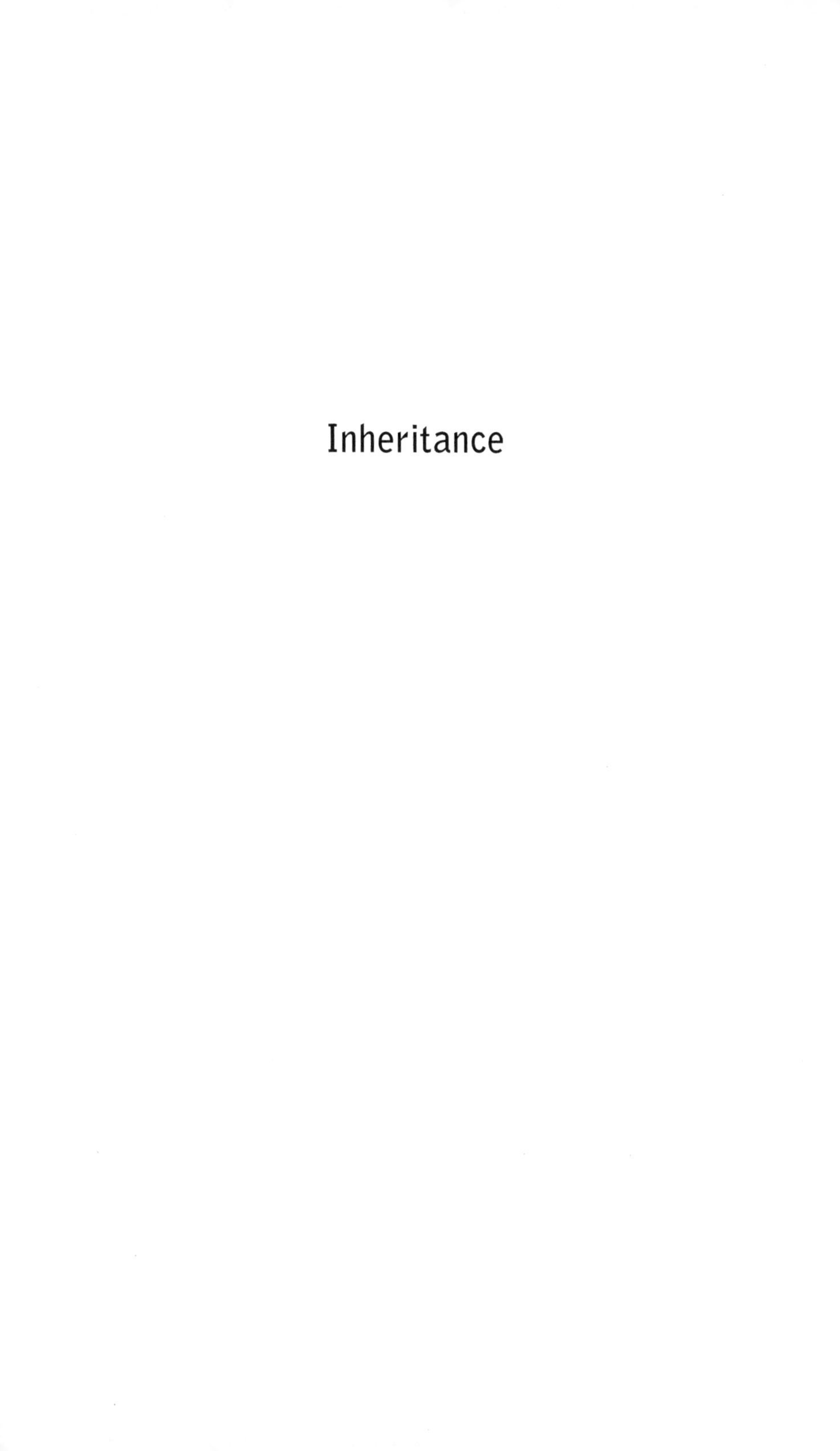

Inheritance

Ancestral Signs

The habit of dying to oneself
has its beginnings in lines
lost to the albatross

beginningless
dreamless
disappears the sail
down the horizon
the sailor the boat the sea

who but the writer spies the ghost ship?
the promised presence divagates
yes, & who throws the six indeed?
the Weaver's art of crime & punishment
of fabulist tales locked in the fabric

the word & its spectacle
attic musings of the textual mosaic
the only breathing space
a now a seed in her mouth
a gullet grown tree

ancestral signs parse in mid-raga
disorderly rhyme put on trial
declares its innocence

New Moon

new moon space is blind
nothing in the frame or out
its meditative eye spying sees nothing
but a circle and its precrust edge
both encase women too dark
with meaning

a reading girl awaits the eye of Shiva
strung out on a bow as arrow and direction
the power of the audience draws the story
along paths never intended
unassisted compositions lie

the moon woman stares into world mirrors
who are the real crustaceans?
a teasing problem you'll agree

the woman of the moon
de-narcissizes the wheel's circle
desire and terror come swishing
through mildewed leaves
a sushumna *tierce de picardie*

Rasa

She dances, he sculpts
Popular movie magic *Chitralekha ... Amrapali*
While we dream temple walls vibrate
With anahata

This is she, Shivakami
Wrapped across his heaving shoulders
Dropping globs of her flesh all over the globe
As her Shiva leaves sculptural motifs
On the gopuras north and south

What supports the figure?
This dancing with his dead wife on his shoulders
What rasa is awakened dancing on death?

A glob of her flesh drops searing yellow
A karana linking dance and geometry
With the love of man and woman
A nrtta aesthetically pleasing
In the independent moves of the torso

Haunted by elements of Hindu iconography
The dancer's knees bend right angles to the audience
Watch her lift that ear-ring off the floor unashamedly woman
Performing the foot requirements for the variations
Possible in particular legends

Feet are fundamental in proving
No love is anatomically impossible
For the woman danced to death
To the cadence of falling flesh

Dark and wonderful she moves
Still a poet's delight and inspiration
In the poet's mind connecting is goddess
Sacrifice and power the dance masters sculpt
Wielding the bow and shooting the arrows
That support the figure in the battlefield

What Dreams May Come

It's night it's winter and the heart squeezes into a tennis ball
turned inside out, furry side in, smooth out
many faceted longing to throw itself into the fire

Sita's fire, that audacious pernicious fire of warriors and priests
powers that haunt like yesterday's ghosts
the same telling in torn armour and frock
The breath of life's tired surfing awakens no response
on the other side of the chalked edge

Sight simultaneous the black rain beneath a clear blue sky
not separated in time or space slowly spinning
the soil brown like a ferris wheel prompt
of the world's turning on its axis

Imprisons the spectator
in her drowning no stopping place
down, down the spell binds the entrance and the exit
in one enduring dive more frieze than urn

More bardo than frieze what dreams may come
what gods or crustaceans to peer through the glass
and its attendant grins
merely subjective visions out of the wheel?

When one is cast off another takes its place
in the recycled nemesis of Greek tragedy
Like Socrates we practise dying
as ontological proof
for the meditating rock

The Purple Rose of Cairo

Her misfortune is without its like
Rainbows scanning chaos stop movement in time
A siren grin reappears
The cat that sat on the mat has become a serious artist
No word is whole no word is without

Thought experiments from Vedanta to Tao
Make the purple rose of Cairo an elsewhere
A bubble universe flying apart in the white of the eye

Enamoured of Vedic words in vermillion
The hiranya-garbha births itself
The concrete body of Ishwara is expanding
With elephantiasis

The absurd potential of words
Nothing is meant by this except kinds of association
A feature selection quite indifferent to relevance
Untamed thinking anthills all this unnecessary order

Mind imitating itself
Take x a spatial code & y a time code
You'll see for pete's sake
What failures of meaning we get into

So what's a good poem?
The answer wind-weary lies
At the bottom of Lake Mansarovar

Saints & Sinners

On the field at Kurukshetra
two armies face each other
Arjuna warrior par excellence quakes
begs Krishna to let him off
Arjuna'd rather give up a kingdom
than murder in war his kinsmen

I am the murderer
God incarnate declares
the universe is unfolding as it should
do your dharma as a kshatriya
you will not kill the atman

weapons do not reach it
flame does not burn it
nor water wet it
wind does not dry it

Ashvattha is the name
Krishna gives the tree of transmigration

Its roots in Heaven its branches on Earth
it hangs head downwards
& calls poets drunk on Soma to sing
the joys awaiting warriors in Indra's Paradise
where Yudhisthira & Duryodhana learn to live
without the illusion of Good & Evil

Patterns of negation
I don't believe the universe is eternal
nor do I believe it is not eternal
or that it is both eternal & not eternal
or that it is neither eternal nor not eternal

The word and the world
feed on each other

Inheritance

cummings keeps the stars apart
        with his mantric words
etched on my heart
        their imprint

on the banks of the Yamuna
        he plays his flute
his smile floats merrily
        dodging marigolds & excrement

my heart
        no one carries in theirs
it floats disembodied
        nursing its inheritance

Stirring Dull Roots

I

The concreted banks
hold back turgid waters
plied by dreaming minds
going too far back in time
like de Kooning's *door to the river*
flowing past to present
in a burst of yellow

no way but this to fill
the hours curved back in themselves
imitating serpents in time & space
outside the mind dissolving

floors of memory & a thousand
furnished rooms

unredeemable footfalls
of the poet with Autumn in her pen
weaving sunlight beyond the mores

stirring dull roots Virginia lay
drowning

II

Mouthful of mantras
yet no images in black light
best possible light suspended
on strings

metaphors pocket falling stars
many dying before their time

always the persuasion
poetry & ash

& memory
a positional colourist
peels back in elegant mauve
what we had
& what we lost

III

Metaphors hurt
shining in their own light
touched by many such
still no face

her body dismembers
arms & legs lope off
her voice swallows
her throat

finally only a mound
perhaps Beckett, heart-shaped
& twinkling bright
would grace the mound
some starry night

81

tap her on her armless shoulder
& ask

does this force you
to think about language?

IV

The old song goes
you can charm the critics
& still have nothin' to eat
the memory of that song
seeks to re-evaluate radical strokes
anchors its ironic frame
to the cracked place of poetry
its pure eye drowns
does not hang in the swell
like the Black Madonna
set afloat in waters of origin & ash
where *Il Postino's* world
is a metaphor
for somethin' else

ash mounds up
making mountains
& moving them

Art choosing landscape
accommodates the pure land

Landscapes

Telling Our Own Stories, Civic Centre Bridge, Wellington

I

Tell me, City of Action
Who owns a story?
By Lauris Edmond's injunction
I can't live here by Chance
I have to Verb and Vibe
Or else fail you
My migrating soul
Tumble dries in circles
On this bridge of Egyptian echoes
My brain washed clean
Of all desire to appropriate
Gasps: what if Shakespeare
Had been so constricted?

II

Beshrew my heart mapped
Vicariously on unseen steps
I rise and fall trapped
The wairua in your winds
Of four directions
Blow and enthrall all
Who come and are conquered
Tell me, City of Artful Winds
Whose stories?

85

III

Washed out of the hair
Gargled out with toothpaste
Scraped off the plate
Dumped in the bin
The question remains
Why *not* live here by chance
Perchance to dream
The word freed
From thorny stubble flanking
The Desert Road

Chendor Beach

It was so smooth the road to freedom
as smooth as the sand I scoop
lying in wait for the turtles

All along Chendor Beach
expectant bodies lay cradled
in sand shorn of identity
a collective quest for a poetic vision
the promise of allegory

Out of the dawn-grey sea they emerge
prehistoric creatures
carrying the sins of the world
on their reincarnate backs

Grunting & heaving they inch their way
less than a feet from our greedy gaze
torch-lit in eerie luminescence

Scaly paws dig snug graves
in single-minded absorption
oblivious to our ecstatic cries

Hung perilous forever
mid-air & frozen
on a Kierkegaardian leap

The eggs are laid
the turtles grunt back to the reddening sea
they do not look back

The Third Country

Colombo
fine dining
& whining
a cinnamon garden
no longer fragrant

Galle
a gem
the sea aquamarine
swims in moonstones

Katharagama
the god of war
heals a boy's hand
plunged in play
boiling rice porridge

Cave, Dambulla
the Buddha reclines
at ease with Vishnu
& Katharagama

Sigiriya
a rock fortress
frowns on fratricidal war
& smiles on asparas
in mirrored graffiti

Ritigula

Hanuman leaps
his tail on fire
brings on war

Anuradhapura

war returns
on the rubble of viharas
& dagobas
on serene hemispheres
of moonstone rock
on Sangamitta's
Bodhi tree

Polonnaruwa

a second war-
abandoned city
Parakrama's sea dries up
in your throat

Trincomalee

a fort not of rock
Portuguese & Dutch
French & British
spray or bray
we've been here

& here my pilgrimage halts
entry to Jaffna denied
a skirmish has begun

Jaffna

my parents' birthplace
a mystery

Samanalakande

Adam set foot here
Buddha left his footprint
butterflies come here
        to die

Lindis Pass

Handed moments like this
Driving through Lindis Pass
Washed hot gold
& blinded with cathedral wonder
Interior red seas sand-dune ribbed backs
Opening old wounds in new ways
Deep into the *biblical desolation*
Of Baxter's crouching tigers
Earnscleugh tailings
& immigrant angst
Foreignness peels away
Forms kinship with metamorphic rock
Rising in agony at times in ecstasy no doubt
Its schistic collision geological eons ago
& still rising a millimeter a year
A landscape in crisis calling forth
Thompson's holy Lindisfarne
For succour

Repulse Bay

named & renamed
this *Shallow Water Bay*

where Tin Hau casts her merciful eyes
over fish & folk

fish as in surplus the Old Man of the Sea rides
his prosperous belly rolling rich in folds

round the *The Bay of a Thousand Years*
dreams of longevity engraved

a hundred gold characters
a teasing alphabet magic

for doubleplusgood returns
on *Greenside Beach* where mainlanders

walk hand-in-glove
over the Bridge of Long Life

then embrace the finality
of the British *Repulse Bay* in the curve

of a Mona Lisa smile Kuan Yin smiles
seated serene on her black lotus

her eyes downcast
on this sandy grotto

The Cairnmuir Terraces

of Bannockburn
hot and dry
ripe plum-hued
fold and unfold
generous brush strokes
yet crafty and minimal
smooth sun-drenched
no leaf to pick
no shade to succour
yet dark hollows deep
with buried histories
of pilgrim miners

      age
with the telling

below the Terraces
fine vines
of central Otago
ululate ripe
for the picking
the promise arcs
in flute stunning lift

Cathedral Square, Christchurch

restless pigeons
looking for a place to anchor

performing against silence
dancing a circus
nudging forcing
my swollen tongue
to give shape

what cannot be said
surrenders

the Chalice is empty
holds nothing
promises nothing

The Cathedral

a fallen body
strains against scaffolds
this press-given emblem
for *Decades of Quakes*

once the classical paradigm
of early settlers
a city's pride
now a motif of disaster

a repeated onslaught
hurting eyes and heart
a trope in the process
of looking picture perfect
for Goethe's frozen music
made literal

its body assigned
to the bookshelf of History
the cathedral humbly reflects
the long white cloud
is what it is
a bold metaphor

Shape-Shifter Landscapes

A faceless habitat sits on floating lines
Curved sensuousness
Primeval land free of bungling humanity

They sang the same song
Towards the unforgiving shore
An endless chorus mellifluous in repetition
Wisdom sought in highs & lows

A majestic tor stands sentinel
Gritty tailings from abandoned mines
Pale sweaty arms raised in the act
Scrub cutting gum digging

The way back long & arduous
As the way in

Abandoned Geography

she's been in this silence for a long time
too many journeys to nowhere
her body her only home

the absence continues
lingers in every doorway
every footpath

the nor'wester whizzes through
all the gaps left unwritten on the body
of the aching land

released from the contested space
of re-arrivals she stands

both asleep and awake
no longer dreaming

only a trace of a woman
in abandoned geography

Notes

Mission Bay to St Heliers

Meant to be read as a long poem of 9 parts. Explores the "narrative of assimilation", what Bharati Mukherjee calls the engagement with "the cultural temporality" of the new land. The protagonist, an immigrant artist, enacts this engagement in her walk from Mission Bay to St Heliers, assimilating the mythological and colonial history of this coastline with her own literary and cultural inheritance.

Lament
Po, po, po Wairaka i raru ai: "The night Wairaka was deceived".

Apakura's lament for the murder of her kinsmen, is likened to "the endless weeping of the waves on the shore".

History & Cultural Relativity
Ka whawhai tonu ake! Ake! Ake!: "We will fight forever. Forever! Forever!"

He wea nei hoki au ka pakaru rikiriki: "I am as a canoe shattered into fragments upon the beach".

Person & Place
Taurere: The Maori name for St Heliers in Haami Bradford's *Mate Tau. Traditional Maori Love Stories*. (1997)

Te Ahu Ki Turangaimua: "The Place Where Turanga Fell"

He hono tangata e koro e mohi: "A human bond cannot be severed"

In Medias Res
die gestundetete: mortgaged time.

Ch'u Yuan: Chinese poet, who wrongfully charged
with treason, drowned himself in the sea, and who is
commemorated during the Dragon Boat Festival.

Ilanko: 5th century Indian poet-prince, whose epic poem, the
Cilapaðikaram ("Lay of the Anklet") tells the tragic story
of Kovalan, his wife, Kannaki (later deified as a Goddess)
and his mistress, Matavi. Considered a Tamil masterpiece,
the *Cilapaðikaram* is also a record of the socio-political and
cultural landscape of three South Indian kingdoms, the
Chola, the Pantiya and the Chera kingdoms.

Tradition & the Poet II

Arunðhati: the Morning Star, symbol of chastity and the
perfect wife.

Zerschreiben!: "Unwrite!"

Caminataiyar, Tankaiya, Pukalenti, Paratitacan and *Karunaniti*
are Tamil poets/dramatists/politicians who re-visioned
Ilanko's *Cilapaðikaram*.

St Heliers

Bhishma: The revered elderstatesman and grandsire of
both the Pandavas and the Kauravas in the Hindu epic,
Mahabharata. Bhishma reluctantly fought on the side of the
Kauravas and lay dying on a bed of arrows until the sun
turned north.

Gallery Talk

Flaubert's Drum

Refers to Flaubert's comment: "Human language is like
a cracked kettle on which we beat our tunes for bears to
dance to, when all the time we long to move the stars to
pity".

Strings

Ist January 2003
Gayatri mantra: A prayer for enlightenment, often recited at dawn, as the first rays of the sun appear.

You're on Earth. There's no cure for it: From Beckett's *Endgame*.

Eo fis
Eo fis: "The Salmon of Knowledge". Odin the Viking God, hung himself, head downwards, as a sacrifice on The World Tree, to gain knowledge of the runic symbols used in divination.

Netting in Hong Kong
Octopus: The local name for the Hong Kong Underground Train System. Hong Kong's seven million people crowd into these trains in their daily commuting to work and back.

Adding one inch to an anonymous mountain refers to an art exhibition in 2000 by China's East Village artists.

Nets: Native English Teachers recruited from all over the world by the Hong Kong Education Department.

A Koan for Hari
butterfly question: Refers to the 4th century Chinese philosopher who woke up from a dream wondering "if he was Chuang Chou who had dreamed he was a butterfly or a butterfly dreaming he was Chuang Chou".

essence or existence question: A question from Kierkegaard's Christian Existentialism.

onehandclapping question: A riddle question (koan) in Zen Buddhism to teach the limits of rational thinking.

what's the answer? what's the question?: Supposedly the last words of Gertrude Stein as she lay dying.

Who Said What

Kowhai Gold
replies Yudhisthira: Refers to a dialogue in the *Mahabharata* between Yudhisthira and Lake Mansarovar.

The Tree in its Setting
I whanau te kauri i konei: "The kauri was born here".

identity by location, stories by relocation: quote from Shashi Tharoor, novelist.

The Tree of Heaven
Qui tollis peccata mundi?: "Who takes away the sins of the world?"

Waking Up in Stanley Place, Akaroa
Mandelstam's verb on horseback: From Osip Mandelstam's *Journey to Armenia*. "What tense would you choose to live in? I want to live in the imperative of the future passive participle – in the 'what ought to be'. I like to breathe that way. That's what I like. It suggests a kind of mounted, bandit-like equestrian honour. That's why I like the glorious Latin *gerundive* – it's a verb on horseback."

Et in Arcadia ego: "Here I am in Paradise".

Inheritance

Ancestral Signs
Raga: A melodic order which together with *tala* (a time cycle) forms the basis of Indian music.

<u>New Moon</u>
Sushumna: The spinal chord.

tierce de picardie: A sudden feeling of bliss.

<u>Rasa</u>
This poem refers to two stories about Lord Shiva and his
consort, Shivakami. Angry with her father for insulting
Shiva, Shivakami kills herself. Shiva goes into *tandava*
(a dance of anger). As Shiva dances in rage, bits of
Shivakami's flesh fall on different parts of India. As legend
goes, temples were built where Shivakami's flesh fell. A
metaphorical claim for the sacred power invested in Hindu
temples.

The second story refers to a dance of competition between
Shiva and Parvathi (the reincarnated Shivakami). It is an
evenly matched contest, until Parvathi 's ear-ring drops.
Shiva, without missing a beat, picks it up with his toes and
raises his leg with it – a dance pose, Parvathi being woman
and modest, is unable to execute.

Chitralekha, Amrapali: Legendary court dancers in ancient
India made popular in Hindi movies.

anahata: Unstruck sound.

rasa: The aesthetic or emotional relish a work of art evokes.

gopuras: Soaring pyramidal towers of Hindu temples.

karanas: Prescribed hand and feet movements in Bharata
Natyam, the classical dance system of South India.

nrtta: Mime in Bharata Natyam.

<u>*What Dreams May Come*</u>
Sita: The wife of Lord Rama in the Hindu epic *Ramayana*, who steps out of the chalk circle drawn for her protection, and is kidnapped by Ravana, King of Lanka.

<u>*The Purple Rose of Cairo*</u>
Vedanta: Hindu philosophy.

hiranya-garbha: The Cosmic Egg in Hindu Creation myths.

Iswara: One of the many names for God.

Lake Mansarovar: The legendary Lake of Enlightenment in the Himalayas.

<u>*Saints & Sinners*</u>
Kurukshetra: The battlefield in the *Mahabharata,* where the Kauravas fought their cousins, the Pandavas.

Arjuna: One of the five Pandavas, a warrior hero.

Krishna: An avatar of Lord Vishnu, born to rid the world of Evil.

Kshatriya: One who belongs to the warrior caste.

Soma: A drink mentioned frequently in the *Rig Veda* as a "messenger of the Gods". One assumes it had a narcotic effect and was an aid to visionary wisdom.

Indra: King of the Gods who rules the Hindu Heaven.

Yudhisthira: The eldest of the Pandava brothers, who is represented as the embodiment of Truth.

Duryodhana: The eldest of the Kauravas, who ignored everyone's advice and embarked on a war with the Pandavas.

At the end of the *Mahabharata*, when all are dead, Yudhisthira goes to Heaven and is shocked to find Duryodhana, his evil cousin, there, while his four brothers, wife and other kinsmen who fought on his side, were in Hell. When Yudhisthira chooses to live in Hell with those he loves, the illusion of Heaven and Hell, Good and Evil, falls away and Yudhisthira attains "the state of the Gods".

Landscapes

Chendor Beach
Chendor Beach in Malaysia is where the Giant Turtles go to lay their eggs, ogled by tourists and the natives.

The Third Country
Kataragama: Another name for the Hindu God Skanda (Sanskrit) or Muruga (Tamil). It is also the name of an important pilgrimage site for Hindus and Buddhists in Sri Lanka.

viharas: Buddhist complex of shrine, congregational hall and the monks' living quarters.

dagobas: Buddhist monuments containing relics of the Buddha or a Buddhist saint. Also called a *stupa*.

Parakrama's sea: An irrigation project, a 2500 hectare tank, built by King Parakrama I (1153-1186).

Sangamitta: The daughter of Emperor Asoka of India who brought a sapling of Buddha's Bodhi Tree to Sri Lanka.

Repulse Bay
Repulse Bay in Hong Kong has had four name changes. Its original name in Chinese translates as 'Shallow Water Bay'. Its second name, 'The Bay of a Thousand Years',

is engraved in gold-painted Chinese characters in a pavilion on this beach. The Japanese, when they captured this beach, called it, rather pragmatically in Japanese, 'Greenside Beach'. When the British repulsed the Japanese here, the Beach became 'Repulse Bay'.

Tin Hau: The Goddess of the Sea to whom fishermen prayed for a bountiful catch.

Kuan Yin: The Goddess of Mercy.